L·O·S·T F·O·R·E·V·E·R

EXTINCT
ANIMALS OF THE
SOUTHERN CONTINENTS

Barbara J. Behm and Jean-Christophe Balouet

Gareth Stevens Publishing
MILWAUKEE

For a free color catalog describing Gareth Stevens' list of high-quality books and multimedia programs, call 1-800-542-2595 (USA) or 1-800-461-9120 (Canada).
Gareth Stevens Publishing's Fax: (414) 225-0377.
See our catalog, too, on the World Wide Web: http://gsinc.com

The editor would like to extend special thanks to Jan W. Rafert, Curator of Primates and Small Mammals, Milwaukee County Zoo, Milwaukee, Wisconsin, for his kind and professional help with the information in this book.

Library of Congress Cataloging-in-Publication Data available upon request from publisher. Fax (414) 225-0377 for the attention of the Publishing Records Department.

ISBN 0-8368-1527-0

This North American edition first published in 1997 by
Gareth Stevens Publishing
1555 North RiverCenter Drive, Suite 201
Milwaukee, Wisconsin 53212 USA

This edition © 1997 by Gareth Stevens, Inc. Based on the book *Extinct Species of the World,* © 1990 by David Bateman, Ltd. (English Language Edition) and © 1989 by Editions Ouest-France (French Language Edition), with original text by Jean-Christophe Balouet and illustrations by Eric Alibert. This edition published by arrangement with David Bateman, Ltd. Additional end matter © 1997 by Gareth Stevens, Inc.

Picture Credits
Eric Alibert: pp. 6, 7, 10, 12 (bottom), 13, 14 (bottom), 20, 22, 25, 28; British Museum of Natural History: Cover, pp. 17, 18, 19; Explorer: p. 8; Jacana: pp. 14 (top), 24; R. Landin: title, pp. 9, 26, 27; National Library: pp. 5, 15, 16, 21, 23; © Zoological Society of London: 11

Series editor: Patricia Lantier-Sampon
Series designer: Karen Knutson
Additional picture research: Diane Laska
Map art: Donna Genzmer Schenström, University of Wisconsin-Milwaukee Cartographic
     Services Laboratory
Series logo artwork: Tom Redman

Printed in the United States of America

1 2 3 4 5 6 7 8 9 01 00 99 98 97

INTRODUCTION

For millions of years, during the course of evolution, hundreds of plant and animal species have appeared on Earth, multiplied, and then, for a variety of reasons, vanished. We all know of animals today — such as the elephant and the rhinoceros, the mountain gorilla and the orangutan — that face extinction because of irresponsible human activity or changes in environmental conditions. Amazingly, hundreds of species of insects and plants become extinct before we can even classify them. Fortunately, in modern times, we are beginning to understand that all living things are connected. When we destroy a plant species, we may be depriving the world of an amazing cure for human diseases. And we know that if we destroy the forest, the desert creeps forward and the climate changes, wild animals die off because they cannot survive the harsh conditions, and humans, too, face starvation and death. Let us remember that every creature and plant is part of a web of life, each perfect, each contributing to the whole. It is up to each of us to end the destruction of our natural world before it becomes too late. Future generations will find it hard to forgive us if we fail to act. No matter what our age or where we live, it is time for every one of us to get involved.

Dr. Jane Goodall, Ethologist

CONTENTS

Words that appear in the glossary are printed in **boldface** type the first time they occur in the text.

SOUTHERN CONTINENTS

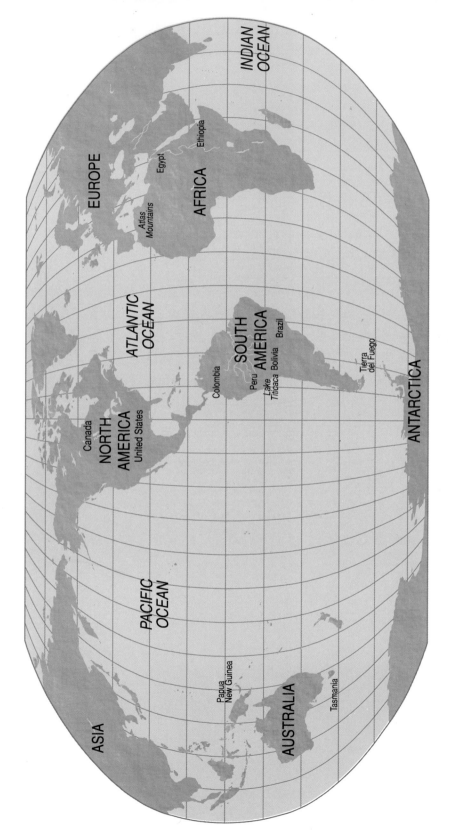

▲ Many species of plant and animal life on Earth have become extinct, and many more species are in imminent danger. This tragic situation is not limited to any one place; it is a global problem. From the northern and southern continents to the islands of Earth's oceans and seas, numerous animal species have disappeared forever. Only the intervention of human resources may now be able to save currently endangered animals. This map indicates some of the continents, countries, bodies of water, and other areas referred to in *Lost Forever: Extinct Animals of the Southern Continents.*

A Vast Continent

Africa is home to a great variety of wildlife, from the **endangered** gorillas and elephants to the tsetse flies. Through the years, this vast continent and its animals have experienced changes in climate, a loss of natural habitat, and an increase in negative human intervention. This has led to the **extinction** of many of its animal **species**.

▲ A historic view of initiation rites for African lion hunters from a book by explorer Dr. David Livingstone.

Birds

A nightjar, *Caprimulgus ludovicianus*, once lived in Ethiopia but died out at the beginning of the twentieth century. A finch, *Neospiza concolor*, also disappeared in the early 1900s. It lived on the island of São Tomé, off the Guinea coast.

Mammals

Two species of zebras became extinct in less than one hundred years. The quagga, *Equus quagga*, once lived in South Africa. It was very **aggressive** and was often used to guard herds of cattle. When the Boers (people of Dutch or French Huguenot descent) settled in South Africa in the mid-seventeenth century, the quagga was hunted as game to feed servants and workers. Local settlers used quagga skins in their homes, and they also exported them. The last quagga in the wild became extinct in 1878. The last specimen in captivity died in 1883 in the Amsterdam Zoo.

▲ The quagga, *Equus quagga*, was a zebra ancestor that lived in South Africa.

A **subspecies** of Burchell's zebra, *Equus burchelli burchelli*, disappeared about 1910. Its habitat overlapped the quagga's. In comparison, the quagga's coat was browner with fewer stripes on the back, and the Burchell's zebra had white on the legs and tail.

Sivatherium, a close relative of the giraffe, is known only from fossils. Its remains indicate that humans may have hunted it. This, along with climatic changes, may have led to *Sivatherium*'s eventual disappearance.

The Atlas bear, *Ursus arctos crowtheri*, faced extinction due to habitat destruction and hunters with guns. This species found refuge in the Atlas Mountains in

▲ *Sivatherium*, a close relative of the giraffe, is now extinct.

▲ The reasons for the disappearance of the saber-toothed cat remain a mystery.

northwestern Africa before completely disappearing about 1870.

One of the saber-toothed cats, *Megantherion*, lived during the time of the first humans. The reasons for its disappearance remain a puzzle. Climatic changes may have played a role. But the growing scarcity of its **prey**, which humans also hunted, may have contributed greatly to its extinction.

Megalotragus was a species of giant antelope that disappeared during the **Holocene**, or **Recent**, **Epoch**. Some of its **remains** suggest that humans hunted it. However, the dramatic changes in climate that occurred throughout Africa during the **Quaternary Period** may also have played a major role in this animal's extinction.

The blue buck antelope of South Africa, *Hippotragus leucophaeus*, died out in 1799. This animal was probably the first African species to become extinct due to hunting by settlers. Early settlers called it the blue goat because it resembled a goat, especially with its goatee beard and curved

▲ *Megalotragus*, a giant antelope, died out during the Holocene Epoch.

horns, and its blue-gray color. Settlers could easily approach and kill the blue buck antelope because the animal did not run from humans.

The Cape hartebeest, *Alcelaphus caama caama*, once found in South Africa, became extinct because of hunting by people and dogs. This gazelle was plentiful in Cape Town in about 1800, but it disappeared rapidly after that time.

The Barbary lion, *Panthera leo barbarus*, became extinct in 1922. Along with the Cape lion, the Barbary lion was the largest of all the lions. Its habitat once covered most of northern Africa, but it became restricted to Tunisia, Algeria, and Morocco during the colonization of that area. The final members of this species died out in the early twentieth century, perhaps because of gunfire during civil wars in Morocco.

▲ The blue buck antelope, *Hippotragus leucophaeus*, was probably the first African species to become extinct at the hands of humans.

▲ The Barbary lion, *Panthera leo barbarus*, had a huge mane that covered half its body.

The Cape lion, *Panthera leo melanochaitus*, died out in South Africa around 1865. Observers described it as having the head of a bulldog, a black mane, and a tuft of black hair under its belly.

Today, Africa contains some of the world's most endanger-ed species. These include the gorilla, *Gorilla gorilla*; the addax antelope, *Addax nasomaculatus*; the Ethiopian ibex, *Capra walie*; and the African elephant, *Loxodonta Africana*. Hunting and **poaching** are greatly reducing the populations of many African species.

▲ Australian Aborigines with ritual face and body decorations.

ABORIGINES AND MARSUPIALS

Humans called **Aborigines** first inhabited Australia over forty thousand years ago. These early peoples traveled on foot across a land bridge from what is now New Guinea. The earliest visit by Europeans was in 1606 by the Dutch, although evidence of earlier visits by the Portuguese exists. Europeans first arrived in Tasmania (Van Diemen's Land), the large island south of Australia, in 1642. Naturalists began exploring Australia in the 1800s. When Aborigines first set foot in Australia, few native predators roamed the land. The Aborigines introduced the dingo, Australia's wild dog. Extensive destruction of the native wildlife began when the Europeans brought firearms, rabbits, foxes, and other predators to Australia in 1800.

Over the years, the animals of Australia have undergone a remarkable **evolution** that led to a diversity of creatures. The mix includes such unrelated species as moles, hares, and jerboas, as well as the egg-laying platypus. In

▲ The giant boa, *Wonambi naracoortensis*, one of Australia's most magnificent reptiles.

▲ The extinct monitor lizard, *Megalania prisca*, reached a length of 23 feet (7 m).

addition, there are nearly 250 species of **marsupials** in Australia. These animals are unique in that newborns continue their development and receive nourishment after they are born in a pouch that is part of the mother's body.

REPTILES

Two species of reptiles became extinct in Australia, both at the hands of humans. One was a giant boa from southeastern Australia,

Wonambi naracoortensis, which grew to 16 feet (5 meters) long. The other was a giant monitor lizard (goanna), *Megalania prisca*, nearly 23 feet (7 m) long.

BIRDS

Australia is home to more than 650 bird species. Two Australian emu species became extinct before 1850. The black emu of King Island, *Dromaius novaehollandiae minor*, died out in 1824. The other extinct emu, *Dromaius novaehollandiae diemeniamus* of Kangaroo Island, grew slightly larger than the emu of King Island.

Two megapodes of the genus *Progura* disappeared soon after the arrival of the Aborigines, probably because

▲ Australia once had two megapodes of the genus *Progura*. These primitive birds did not sit on their eggs but laid them in a large mass of vegetation. Decomposition provided the heat necessary for the young birds' development.

of predation by dingoes. These birds laid their eggs in a mass of vegetation. The decomposing vegetation provided heat to incubate the babies inside the eggs.

Two parrot species are considered to be extinct. The night parrot, *Geopsittacis occidentalis*, lived in the deserts. The paradise parrot, *Psephotus pulcherrimus*, inhabited Queensland.

▲ The black emu of King Island, *Dromaius novaehollandiae minor*, became extinct in 1824.

MAMMALS

Gilbert's potoroo, or rat-kangaroo, *Potorous gilberti*, lived in marshes and wetlands. Aborigines called it *ngil-gyte*. Rat-kangaroos could reach a length of 2 feet (60 centimeters) from head to tail. They became extinct before 1900.

A related species, *Potorous platyops*, or broad-faced potoroo, was already rare at the time of its discovery in Western Australia. The last known capture occurred in 1908. It became extinct due to the introduction of cats and foxes, and to brush fires. Unlike their smaller relatives, these species did not dig burrows. This could have also led to their extinction.

Zaglossus hacketti, a close relative of the echidna, was a **monotreme** that once inhabited the Australian mainland. Actions of humans

▲ Gilbert's potoroo (rat-kangaroo), *Potorous gilberti*, disappeared before 1900.

▲ The extinct *Zaglossus hacketti*, a close relative of the echidna.

led to *Zaglossus hacketti*'s demise. It was 3 feet (1 m) long and covered with spines. It had hair and a tube-shaped beak and fed on insects.

The extinct freckled marsupial mouse, *Antechinus apicalis*, lived in Western Australia. A fold in its skin and extra-long body hair served as a pouch.

The desert bandicoot, *Perameles eremiana*, lived in the southern and eastern areas of Australia. It disappeared around 1940. Another bandicoot species, *Perameles myosurus*, became extinct by 1910.

The pig-footed bandicoot, *Chaeropus ecaudatus*, had two toes on its front feet like

▲ The extinct freckled marsupial mouse had litters of up to seven young at a time.

▲ This species of bandicoot, *Perameles myosurus*, became extinct in 1910.

a pig. Each hind foot had only one toe. In 1907, only a few survived in the Lake Eyre region of South Australia. They were last seen in 1925.

During prehistoric times, many marsupial species disappeared. The giant forms did not survive the arrival of humans. The largest marsupial skull recorded measured 6.5 feet (2 m). These unique animals had

incisors like those of rabbits and hind legs similar to those of their climbing ancestors. These giant marsupials resembled the rhinoceros or the hippopotamus more than the kangaroo.

Grey's wallaby, *Macropus greyi*, was a small wallaby. It measured a little less than 3 feet (1 m) long and lived in the deforested zones close to the sea and the salt lakes of

▲ The extinct Grey's wallaby, *Macropus greyi*, was a small species often hunted for its skin.

South Australia. It leaped like an antelope, taking a short jump first, then a long one. Humans killed these animals for their skins. The last Grey's wallaby died in the Adelaide Zoo about 1940.

The brown hare-wallaby, *Lagorchestes leporides*, was a small wallaby whose behavior, coat, and ears were similar to the European hare.

The actions of the European fox, brought in to eliminate the excessive rabbit population in Australia at the beginning of the nineteenth century, probably led to the brown hare-wallaby's extinction around 1890.

The thylacine or Tasmanian wolf, *Thylacinus cynocephalus*, had a reputation as a fierce

▲ The coat, ears, and behavior of the extinct brown hare-wallaby, *Lagorchestes leporides*, were similar to the European hare's.

▲ The thylacine, or Tasmanian wolf, *Thylacinus cynocephalus*, at one time lived on mainland Australia, but withdrew to Tasmania as the dingoes increased in number and moved farther into the continent.

predator. It hunted kangaroos, wallabies, and ground-nesting birds with its powerful jaws. Its reputation worsened when it killed sheep and aggressive dogs. Trappers put poisonous bait in their traps to kill thylacines in order to keep them from eating the animals caught in the traps. From 1888 to 1914, the government, along with a private company, paid premiums to people who killed thylacines. This action led to the destruction of over two thousand of these animals. The two last known captures took place between 1930 and 1933, and the final specimen died in a zoo in 1936. Official protection ordered by the Australian government in 1938 was too late to save the thylacine from extinction.

Palorchestes was a giant marsupial that reached up to 12 feet (3.6 m) in height. This incredible animal is known only through fossils. Scientists are sure that *Palorchestes* had a trunk, but nothing is certain about its behavior or diet. It lived during the time of humans, who hunted it into extinction.

TASMANIAN ABORIGINES

Not even human beings are safe from extinction. Until 1876, Aborigines inhabited Tasmania. Today, these humans have disappeared from the island. The Tasmanian Aborigines were a peaceful people who were afraid of the Europeans who invaded their island and who

▲ Extinct *Palorchestes* was a giant marsupial that grew to 12 feet (3.6 m) in height.

▲ Queen Lijiwiji Trucannini, the last Tasmanian Aborigine, died in 1876.

destroyed them with guns and disease. The last known individual, Queen Lijiwiji Trucannini, nicknamed Lalla Rooth, died of natural causes in 1876.

A Land in Peril

Deforestation is creating deserts in much of South America. Hundreds of animal species are endangered today because of human hunting and the destruction of their forest homes.

The chinchilla, *Chinchilla laniger*, still wild at the beginning of the twentieth century, was eliminated from its natural habitat in less than twenty years. Today, this species no longer exists in the wild. It is limited to chinchilla farms, kept alive only because of its profitability to humans.

▲ The chinchilla, *chinchilla laniger*, would have already become extinct except for the fact that it is now raised on farms by humans for profit.

Many South Americans collect monkeys or hunt them for their meat. Many other species of wildlife in South America, such as the uakari or bald-headed monkey, the gold lion tamarin, the Chaco wolf, the Amazonian manatee, the spectacled bear, the pampas deer, the llama, and the vicuna cannot survive much longer without the necessary protection.

Fish

Lake Titicaca, on the frontier between Peru and Bolivia, used to be home to a unique fish, *Orestias cuvieri*. It had a flat head and two large eyes, and it could reach 12 inches (30 cm) in length. It was a major food source for the people living near the lake. In 1937, one hundred years after this fish was discovered, the North American Great Lakes trout, *Salvelinus namaycush*, was introduced to Lake Titicaca. The

▲ The flat-headed fish, *Orestias cuvieri*, died out soon after the North American Great Lakes trout, *Salvelinus namaycush*, was introduced into its habitat.

introduced trout rapidly eliminated the native fish.

BIRDS

The Magdalena tinamou, *Crypturellus saltuarius*, became extinct by 1943 in Colombia.

The tiger heron, *Tigrisoma fasciatus fasciatus*, was last seen in 1912.

The pallid falcon, *Falco kreyenborgi*, native to Tierra del Fuego and known only from five birds, became extinct in 1961.

A subspecies of the yellow-billed pintail duck, *Anas georgica niceforoi*, disappeared in 1952.

A curassow, *Crax fasciolata pinima*, found in Brazil, was last seen in 1952.

MAMMALS

Human settlement of South America dates back about ten thousand years. Indians known as Mayas and Incas were the first inhabitants.

They were of North American origin and crossed the Isthmus of Panama to reach South America.

The presence of humans in South America is so ancient that many human species have disappeared. Only bones, thousands of years old, have been found to prove the existence of these ancient peoples. Human bones have been discovered in the province of Minas Gerais. They were found mixed together with hundreds

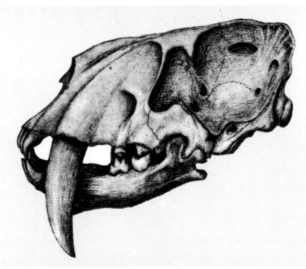

▲ South America was home to many **edentate**, or toothless, mammals, as seen in the remains of this *Megatherium*.

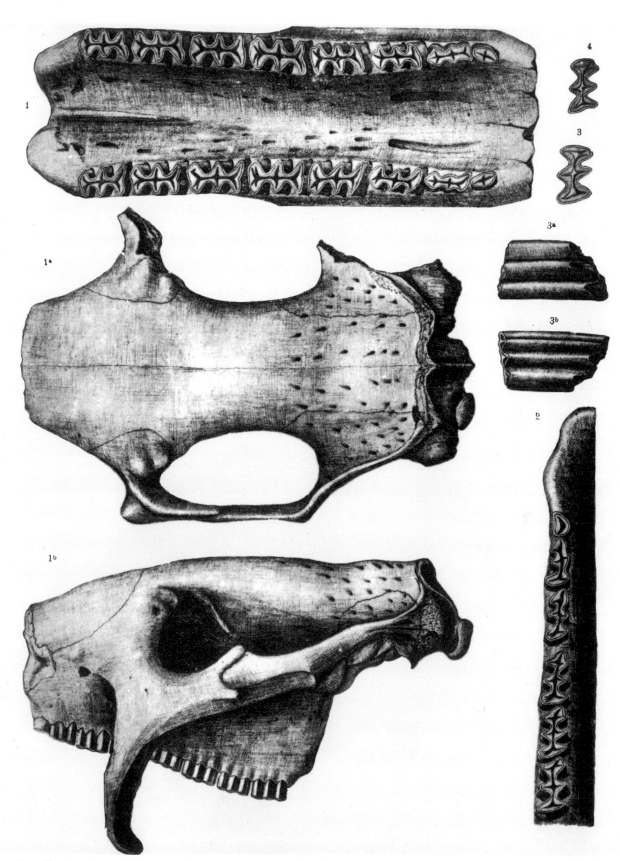

▲ Fossil remains of giant edentate mammals of South America.

of animal bones belonging to at least forty-four species of wildlife that are now extinct.

Among them were two giant edentate mammals, *Mylodon robustus* and *Taxodon platensis*; the giant armadillo, *Glyptodon elegans*; the mastodon, *Mastodon humboldtii*; and the pampas ox, *Bos pamaeus*. Most of the larger animal species in South America disappeared before the arrival of the Europeans in the 1500s.

Today, many South American wildlife species are on the brink of extinction. Every effort must be made to save natural habitat and stop hunting and poaching so these animals may survive.

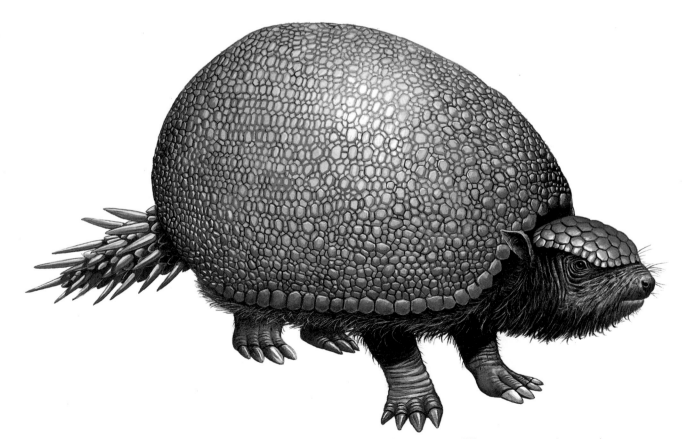

▲ Some shells of the extinct *Glyptodon elegans*, a giant armadillo, grew so large that Indians used them for shelter.

▽△▽△▽△▽△▽△▽△▽△▽△▽△▽△▽△▽△▽△▽△▽△▽△▽△▽△

SCIENTIFIC NAMES OF ANIMALS IN THIS BOOK

Animals have different names in every language. To simplify matters, researchers the world over have agreed to use the same scientific names, usually from ancient Greek or Latin, to identify animals. With this in mind, most animals are classified by two names. One is the genus name; the other is the name of the species to which they belong. Additional names indicate further subgroupings. The scientific names for the animals included in *Lost Forever: Extinct Animals of the Southern Continents* are:

Addax antelope . . . . *Addax nasomaculatus*
African elephant . . . . *Loxodonta Africana*
Atlas bear . . . . *Ursus arctos crowtheri*
Barbary lion . . . . *Panthera leo barbarus*
Black emu . . . *Dromaius novaehollandiae minor*
Blue buck antelope . . . . *Hippotragus leucophaeus*
Broad-faced potoroo . . . . *Potorous platyops*
Brown hare-wallaby . . . . . *Lagorchestes leporides*
Burchell's zebra . . . . . . *Equus burchelli burchelli*
Cape hartebeest . . . . . . *Alcelaphus caama caama*
Cape lion . . . . . . *Panthera leo melanochaitus*
Chinchilla . . . . *Chinchilla laniger*
Curassow . . . . *Crax fasciolata pinima*
Desert bandicoot . . . . *Perameles eremiana*
Echidna (early relative of) . . . . . *Zaglossus hacketti*
Edentates . . . . . *Megatherium, Mylodon robustus,*
. . . . *Taxodon platensis*
Ethiopian ibex . . . . *Capra walie*
Finch . . . . *Neospiza concolor*
Flat-headed fish . . . . *Orestias cuvieri*
Freckled marsupial mouse . . . *Antechinus apicalis*
Giant antelope . . . . *Megalotragus*
Giant armadillo . . . . *Glyptodon elegans*
Giant boa . . . . *Wonambi naracoortensis*
Giant marsupial . . . . *Palorchestes*

Gilbert's potoroo (rat-kangaroo) . *Potorous gilberti*
Giraffe (early relative of) . . . . *Sivatherium*
Gorilla . . . . *Gorilla gorilla*
Grey's wallaby . . . . *Macropus greyi*
Kangaroo Island emu . . . .
. . . . *Dromaius novaehollandiae diemeniamus*
Magdalena tinamou . . . . . . *Crypturellus saltuarius*
Mastodon . . . . *Mastodon humboldtii*
Megapodes . . . . *Progura*
Monitor lizard . . . . *Megalania prisca*
Night parrot . . . . *Geopsittacis occidentalis*
Nightjar . . . . *Caprimulgus ludovicianus*
North American Great Lakes trout . . . .
. . . . *Salvelinus namaycush*
Pallid falcon . . . . *Falco kreyenborgi*
Pampas ox . . . . *Bos pamaeus*
Paradise parrot . . . . *Psephotus pulcherrimus*
Pig-footed bandicoot . . . . . . *Chaeropus ecaudatus*
Quagga . . . . *Equus quagga*
Saber-toothed cat . . . . *Meganthereon*
Thylacine (Tasmanian wolf)
. . . . *Thylacinus cynocephalus*
Tiger heron . . . . *Tigrisoma fasciatus fasciatus*
Yellow-billed pintail duck . . . .
. . . . *Anas georgica niceforoi*

GLOSSARY

Aborigines — original inhabitants of an area.

aggressive — quick to attack or start a fight.

edentate — an animal without teeth.

endangered — in peril or danger of dying out, or becoming extinct.

evolution — the process of changing shape or developing gradually over a long period of time.

extinction — the dying out of all members of a plant or animal species.

Holocene, or Recent, Epoch — the span of time that began about ten thousand years ago, a subdivision of the (current) Quaternary Period.

marsupials — mammals that have a pouch on the abdomen of the females to carry and nourish the young.

monotremes — egg-laying mammals in the scientific order Monotremata, which includes the duckbills and echidnas.

poaching — the illegal capture or killing of animals.

prey — an animal that is eaten by other animals for food.

Quaternary Period — the current period, which began 2.5 million years ago.

remains — a skeleton, bones, or dead body.

species — a group of animals sharing the same physical characteristics.

subspecies — a further subdivision of the larger species category.

MORE BOOKS TO READ

Animal Extinctions: What Everyone Should Know. R. J. Hoage, ed. (Smithsonian)

The Doomsday Book of Animals: A Natural History of Vanished Species. (Penguin)

Endangered! (series). Bob Burton (Gareth Stevens)

Environment Alert! Vanishing Rain Forests. Paula Hogan (Gareth Stevens)

The Extinct Species Collection (series). (Gareth Stevens)

In Peril! (series). Barbara J. Behm and J-C Balouet (Gareth Stevens)

VIDEOS

African Wildlife. (National Geographic)

The Amazing Marsupials. (Australian Ark)

Search for the Great Apes. (National Geographic Video)

World Safari. (Wildlife in Action)

WEB SITES

http://envirolink.org/

http://netvet.wustl.edu/wildlife.htm

PLACES TO WRITE

The following organizations educate people about animals, promote the protection of animals, and encourage the conservation of natural habitat. Include a self-addressed, stamped envelope for a reply.

International Wildlife
    Coalition
70 East Falmouth Highway
East Falmouth, MA 02536

Canadian Wildlife
    Federation
2740 Queensview Drive
Ottawa, Ontario K2B 1A2

World Wildlife Fund
1250 24th Street, N.W.
Washington, D.C. 20037

International Fund for
    Animal Welfare
P.O. Box 56
Paddington, New South
    Wales 2021
Australia

Greenpeace
1436 U Street, N.W.
Washington, D.C. 20009

International Fund for
    Animal Welfare
P.O. Box 2587
Rivonia 2128, South Africa

Canadian Nature
    Federation
One Nicholas Street
Suite 520
Ottawa, Ontario K1N 7B7

Department of
    Conservation
P.O. Box 10-420
Wellington, New Zealand

Royal Society for the
    Prevention of Cruelty
    to Animals
3 Burwood Highway
Burwood East
Victoria 3151
Australia

National Wildlife
    Federation
8925 Leesburg Pike
Vienna, VA 22184

Earth Watch
17167 Tam O'Shanter
    Drive
Poway, CA 92064

ACTIVITIES TO HELP SAVE ENDANGERED SPECIES

1. Contact a nature organization in your area. Ask how you can become involved in helping save wildlife.

2. Contact a wildlife rehabilitation center in your area and find out what educational programs or activities they offer to the public.

3. Visit an exhibit at a natural history museum where there are replicas of extinct animals. Or spend a day at the zoo. Are any of the animals you see endangered?

4. Educate others about what you have learned concerning extinct animals, as well as endangered animals and endangered habitats.

5. Write to government officials to express your support of strengthening the Endangered Species Act.

INDEX